CREWEL EMBROIDERY

Fay Anderson

Frontispiece: Hand Bag, see page 38

Introductory instructions by
Margaret Beautement

This edition first published 1977 by
Octopus Books Limited
59 Grosvenor Street, London W1

Copyright © 1977 Octopus Books Ltd

ISBN 0 7064 0638 9

Produced and printed in Hong Kong by
Mandarin Publishers Limited
22A Westlands Road, Quarry Bay

Contents

Introduction

The word 'crewel' describes the highly spun, two-ply wool with which the embroidery is stitched. But crewel embroidery is a deceptively simple term for a richly varied style of embroidery that flourished from about the mid-seventeenth century to the mid-eighteenth.

The most effective use of crewel embroidery was on bed hangings, where exotic flowers and animals, the Tree of Life theme, unicorns, griffins, fruits, flowing leaves and twining branches curved and twisted in elaborate and colourful designs.

When the art was carried across to America's New England states, it assumed a lighter feel and a greater mellowness of colour. And it became a craft for every housewife who spun her own linen and made her own dyes.

Now the art of crewel embroidery is enjoying a modern-day revival. In this age of industrialization we are rediscovering a craft that had its beginnings over a thousand years ago, and we are relearning how to express creative individualism and talent as our forebears did so successfully.

Whether you are a beginner or an advanced embroiderer, you will find easy-to-follow instructions for all of the full-colour illustrated articles made especially for this book. Most of the designs, both modern and traditional, are adaptable for other pieces you might wish to make. Colour suggestions are given, too, but here again you might want to let your own imagination and taste guide you in your selections.

In any event, we hope that you will find as much joy and satisfaction in working the pieces as this book's contributors did in creating them for you.

Opposite: bedspread, see page 91.

Fabrics

Fabric suggestions are given for each of the designs in this book, but you may like to experiment. Feel free to do so! Any fabric which is firm to handle will support crewel wool stitchery. Your choice can range from twill woven dress cotton to the exciting selection available in curtain fabric departments. When you buy, take a colour choice of crewel wool with you. Compare the weight of wool with the weight of fabric. Try out the effect of the wool against the fabric. If you're not certain whether your choice of material is correct, it's advisable to buy a small piece and embroider a selection of the design on it. If it pleases you and holds the stitches, then buy what you need! Some man-made fibres have a sheen which is too hard to blend happily with the wool. The colours too can be affected by the type of woven thread. Surface stitches with crewel wool are lost on a fabric woven with coarse fibres. The stitches would need to be too thick and heavy. Conversely, the thread would pucker a very fine fabric. A closely woven fabric of medium weight will prove to be the best ground. Design choice will affect choice of fabric. So will the purpose of the finished embroidery. Decide on the design before choosing the fabric. For practical purposes, choose an easy-care fabric. There's a wider choice for pictures and wall-hangings. Embroidery for a dress detail can look equally effective on cotton or wool. A cotton twill would be a suitable weight. Look for smooth rather than slub fabrics. Embroidery adds extra weight, so the fabric must be firm enough to take the weight without spoiling the hang of the dress. A single pocket on a skirt, for example, is better lightly embroidered if the skirt is not to pull unevenly. A continuous border on a skirt or curtain will improve the hang. The weight will add an even pull along the hem.

Needlecraft suppliers stock selections of linens and cottons for different embroidery techniques.

Linen twill is the traditional fabric for crewel work. Cream/natural in colour, it is thick and hard wearing and excellent as an upholstery and curtain fabric. Use a bold pattern to complement the weight of the fabric.

Linen–plain weave. This is pleasant to handle and available in a good range of colours. Small scale designs with fine stitchery stand out clearly on the smooth surface.

Slub weave linen or cotton. The uneven surface will take textured stitchery to advantage. Fine details will be lost on this surface. For a rich effect, you will need two or more strands of yarn in the needle.

Enlarging the Design

Outline drawings are given for each design. Those which need to be enlarged to fit the suggested article are marked with an asterisk. The process for enlarging is a simple one.

Onto a large sheet of tissue or tracing paper mark out the size of the finished design. Divide the space into the same number of vertical and horizontal lines as on the small design.

Transfer the design lines from each small square to the corresponding large square.

It is easier to follow a large design – such as the window blind – if the squares are marked with letters or figures.

For a small fee, the simplest method of all is to have your design enlarged by a photostat concern that handles blueprints and other photostats. You'll save yourself a great deal of time and receive a perfect enlargement.

Pages 12-14 suggest the types of paper to use for the different methods of transferring the design to the fabric.

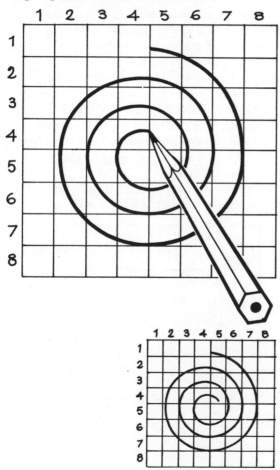

Design to Fabric

Check that the cut edges of the fabric are even by pulling a thread and cutting to the straight weave. Positioning the design correctly onto the fabric is an important part of preparation. It is not difficult and takes little time, but is well worth the small amount of trouble for the pleasure the finished embroidery will give.

Where the embroidery will fill the centre of the fabric, measure and run a basting thread for the vertical and horizontal centres. (For each design, suggestions are given for marking any unusual placing.)

Marking lines may be stitched with basting lines along the straight weave of the fabric or marked with pins.

Use any of the following methods when transferring the design, but be careful with the transfer pencil method, in which the design is pressed on with a hot iron. The pins would mark the fabric, so use the basting method here.

There are four methods of transferring the design to the fabric.

Prick and Pounce Method

You will need:
1. Design drawn onto tracing paper.
2. Fine needle in a cork holder.
3. Fabric pad.
4. Small roll of felt.
5. Powdered tailor's chalk and charcoal.

This is a traditional method used by many craftsmen for transferring a design to a working surface. It is not suitable for a slub or textured weave. The fine needle with the eye end pushed into the cork makes a good pricker.

Lay the embroidery design onto a pad, such as a folded blanket. With the needle, prick holes at regular intervals along the design lines. Space the holes evenly and not too closely or the paper will tear.

Lay the pricked tracing in position on the fabric. Sprinkle with powdered

Diagram 1. Prick and pounce method

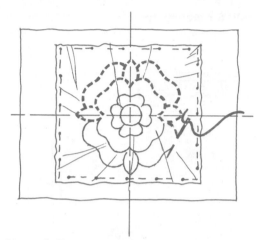

Diagram 2. Tissue paper method

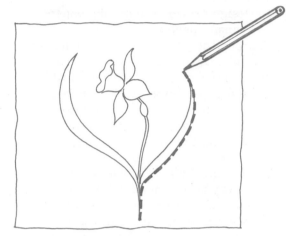

Diagram 3. Transfer pencil method

white tailor's chalk for a dark fabric
–mix in a little crushed charcoal for a
light fabric. Then with a small roll of
felt, rub the powder through the holes.
Carefully remove the tracing paper and,
with a very fine brush and water
colour, paint over the lines of powder.
When the paint is dry, gently shake the
surface powder from the fabric.

Tissue Paper Method
You will need:
1. Design drawn onto tissue paper.
2. Fine sewing needle.
3. Cottons in similar colour to the
   embroidery yarns.
Work on a large, flat surface. Pin the
tissue paper design in position on the
fabric. Outline the design with running
stitches. Make a smaller stitch on the
surface than under the fabric. When
the outlines are complete, remove the
pins and gently tear away the paper
from the sewn lines. The stitched

design keeps its shape if the forefinger
of the left hand holds the stitches flat
as the paper is torn away with the
right hand.
Stitch each design area with a similar
colour to that of the embroidery. You
will find that being able to see where
colour changes occur makes the work
go more quickly.
This method is excellent for marking
simple, bold shapes and the only
satisfactory one for transferring to a
slub fabric.

13

Transfer Pencil

You will need:

1. Design drawn onto tracing paper.
2. Transfer pencil.

Sharpen the pencil to as fine a point as possible. Draw very lightly over the design lines on the wrong side of the tracing paper. Short strokes are better than a continuous line. On a large design, sharpen the pencil several times so that the lines remain fine. *see diagram on preceding page*

The design can now be used in the same way as a commercial transfer. If you want to reverse your design, draw with the pencil on the right side of the tracing paper. The design will iron-on in reverse so make sure you have the transfer line drawn in the correct position for the embroidery. Pin face down onto the fabric and press with a hot iron. *It is important to keep the drawing fine as the line spreads with the heat from the iron.*

Carbon Paper Method

You will need:

1. Dressmaker's carbon paper.
2. Tracing wheel.
3. Design marked onto tracing or tissue paper.

This method is successful with smooth, plain-weave fabrics. Use white carbon for a dark fabric, yellow for a light. Lay the fabric on a smooth surface. Cover the design area with carbon paper, then with the traced design. Take extra care in positioning the design. Make sure it is straight in relation to the grain of the fabric. The carbon paper conceals the grain. Pin

the three layers together. Outline the design with the tracing wheel, pressing firmly for a clear line.

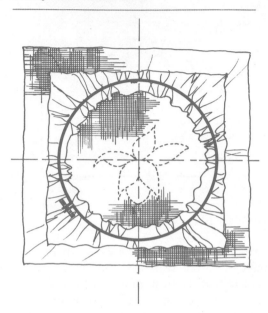

Diagram 1. Using a ring frame; lay tissue paper between the fabric and the outer ring to prevent marks occurring

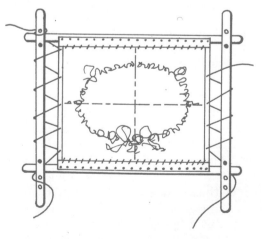

Diagram 2. Fabric laced to sides of frame

Mounting the Fabric

Many stitches may be worked either in the hand or in a frame. Whether you use a frame or not is therefore quite often a matter of personal preference. However, for large, laid work areas a frame is essential. Both hands need to be free to guide the lines of thread and without a frame it is difficult to lay threads and tie them down with any accuracy. The fabric puckers because the thread is too tight, or loose threads are hanging because too much has been left.

If you have not used an embroidery frame before you will find that it takes a little time to accustom yourself to working with one hand above the frame and the other below; but once the skill is acquired, many people prefer working in a frame.

There are two styles of frame: **the slate** or **rectangular embroidery frame**, a rectangle in which the embroidery is mounted and remains for all the stitching; and **the ring frame** or **hoop frame** from which the fabric can be easily moved for quick line stitching. For crewel work **the ring frame** or **hoop frame** is probably the most useful as the surface stitch and laid work areas alternate.

Both hands need to be free. Use either a ring frame with a clamp, or a frame on a small stand which can be used as a lap or table frame.

The top ring with an adjustable screw is removed and the fabric laid over the ring.

see diagram 1

Work with the grain of the fabric vertical and horizontal across the ring. Press the outer ring over the fabric and pull evenly with the horizontal and vertical grain so as not to stretch the fabric out of shape. Pull gently from each side in turn until the fabric is taut. Tighten the adjustable screw.

To prevent the ring from marking the fabric, lay a sheet of tissue paper between the fabric and the outer ring. Tear away the centre working area.

In a **slate frame** the fabric is mounted and remains until the embroidery is complete.

Work at the frame by laying it across two chairs or between a table and chair. It then becomes a level working table. Slate frames vary in style but the basic method of mounting the fabric is the same for all.

Mark the centres of the webbing, which is fixed to the top and bottom rollers. Stitch a strong tape to the sides of the embroidery fabric.

Mark the vertical centre of the fabric. Match the top centres and oversew the fabric to the webbing, working from the centre outward.

Repeat for the opposite end.

Fix the side slats so that the fabric is taut.

Lace the sides of the fabric to the sides of the frame.

see diagram 2

Use a heavy embroidery needle threaded with fine string and stitch into the tape added at the sides and over the side slats of the frame. Work from the centres outward leaving sufficient string to complete the second section of the lacing at each side.

From the centres outward, pull the string until the fabric is taut. Secure the string at the corners.

Colour Choice

Suggestions for colour schemes accompany each design in this book. However, colour choice is completely personal and you may wish to vary the schemes according to your own tastes. If so, take note of the following:

* If you're a beginner, it's best to start slowly. Choose one main colour and gradations of that same colour. Then, if you like, select one other harmonious colour. Most art teachers advise students to start with a limited amount of colours, then gradually, when these are mastered, to add others. It's a good method to follow.

* Observing nature will help to sharpen your colour sense—the subtle changes of green on a tree, various shades of reds and pinks so delicately balanced on a rose, the lush colours in a flower garden, all blending beautifully, and the muted shades of a rainbow. If you examine a rainbow carefully, you'll find a natural harmonious progression of colour—red, orange, yellow, green, blue, indigo, violet. (A hint on how to remember this. Memorize: Richard Of York Gained Battles In Vain.) Each of the colours begins with the same letter of each word (i.e. Richard—red, Of—orange, etc.). If you use gradations of one colour and let these shades blend gradually into the next, you'll find a lovely glowing effect.

* Vary the strength of colour. Whether several or only one or two colours are used, include a very light and a very dark tone among the medium weights of tone. A few white stitches grouped among rich colours will lighten the whole design. A very deep tone in a mainly light-toned embroidery will strengthen and enrich it.

* In planning your choice of thread colours, include the background. In many of these crewel work designs, a proportion of the whole scheme is background. Consider it as part of the whole. A design worked mainly in line with open stitching will take more intense colour than one where the stitching is worked in close rows. Each row strengthens the colour of the next.

* Generally, it's best not to use a colour in one place only on the design and not in another—although there are times when you might want an especially dramatic effect. Then, one colour used on its own will serve that purpose.

* Every colour ranges from light to dark. Some crewel wool ranges include as many as seven or eight variations. So be sure, when buying, to select your colours in daylight and to choose colours that blend with your surroundings.

* Changing the scheme is easy if you note the tone variations as well as the number of colours used in the original design.

* Before making your final decision on colour choice, it's really best to take that extra bit of time to experiment on your design or a quickly-drawn copy with crayons, coloured pencils or water colours. Although the colours won't be exactly the same as the wool you choose, you can get a general idea as to what pleases or displeases you.

There are no hard and fast colour rules. Therefore, the above suggestions are just guidelines to help you discover your own sense of colour harmony.

Opposite: see the wide range of colours available in crewel wool.

Threads and Needles

Crewel wool is a fine, two-ply thread, highly spun to a tight twist. The fineness of the thread makes it versatile to use.

Choose a stitch and work three separate rows of a few inches. Work each row with a different number of strands in the needle, the first with a single thread. The finished effect for each is quite different. The change of scale changes the appearance of the stitch.

Much of the pleasure in embroidery lies in its textural appearance. With the simplest designs and colours and with crewel wool, there is great opportunity for making the most of texture. For maximum effect, alternate thick areas with thin.

A single thread worked on a small design can look very delicate. Equally, several strands and larger stitches will have great impact. It's a question of mood, of matching design to scale, to thread weight, to design content. Approximate amounts of wool and suggestions for the number of strands are given in the text. Crewel wools are available by the ounce, by the cut quarter ounce or by thirty-yard skeins. If Appleton's Crewel wool is unobtainable, any other crewel wool may be substituted.

The 'amount required' in the instructions refers to the number of thirty-yard skeins needed. Each person works to a different tension and you may find that you will need either more or less strands than suggested. Visually, you may find that the embroidery is too thick or too thin for your personal taste. There is no hard and fast rule as to what is right to use. Embroidery is at its best when it makes a clear and definite pattern on the fabric. The final result is disappointing if the overall effect is thin. Work one of the smaller designs first—such as the simple motif on the glasses case—to get the right working tension and the scale of stitching. If crewel wools prove difficult to obtain in the exact colours you require, 2 ply knitting wool can be used but the finished effect will not, of course, be the same.

Crewel needles have a long, narrow eye. Different numbers of strands can be threaded in according to the size of the eye. Choose a needle of sufficient size so that it will slide the thread through the fabric without tugging. This ensures smooth stitching.

Chenille needles have a larger eye, slightly wider than crewel and therefore easier to thread. The smaller sizes are shorter than crewel needles and are easier to handle for working knot and loop stitches.

Tapestry needles have a blunt end and are useful for threaded running and some laid work patterns where the threads are not taken back through the fabric.

Working from the Design

For each of the embroideries shown, an outline drawing is given for the design. The figures on the outline refer to the colour list suggested in the instructions. Stitch symbols are indicated and a key is given for the names of the stitches used.
Notes are given in the instructions where the stitches are worked in an unusual manner.

A selection of counted thread embroideries using crewel wool is given towards the end of the book.
Colour schemes are suggested, but the ideas shown are ideal for using lengths of wool from other projects.

Some of the designs on the following pages are too complicated to enlarge by the methods given on pages 12, 13 and 14. These more complex designs are traditional in crewel embroidery and are well worth the extra effort in working them. The best method for enlarging these designs is to have them done photographically. Architects and engineers' printers will do this for you fairly inexpensively and supply you with a photostat print from which you can make a tracing.

Stitches

Stitches make the texture of embroidery. Relating one type to another creates an intriguing play of light across the surface of the design. The stitches suggested for the designs are cross-referred to the selection shown here, but almost any one suggested can be exchanged for any other. Each has a particular quality to add to the design. The number of strands in the needle affects the size of the stitch—the more strands, the larger the stitch. Work

with a short length of yarn in the needle—about eighteen inches to avoid knotted and rubbed wool.

The stitches are grouped according to their basic method of working. They can be roughly divided into flat, looped and knotted stitches. Laid patterns have elements of all three groups and are listed separately.

Some extra stitches are explained, with the designs on which they have been used, later in the book.

FLAT STITCHES

Work satin, surface satin and long and short stitch in a frame for easy handling and smooth results.

Back stitch ▶

A fine, very flat line.
Bring the needle up from the back and return it to the fabric slightly behind. Bring it out again a little in front of the first stitch and return it at the point where the needle first came through.

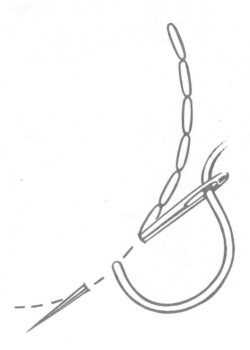

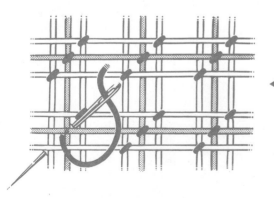

◀ Battlement couching

This is similar to Jacobean couching, only three different colours are used. Lay three lots of even threads horizontally and vertically. Tie down the points of intersection of each lot with small slanting stitches.

20

Couching ▶

A line or filling stitch. Work it in a frame. Take the end of a long piece of yarn through to the back of the fabric. This may be a very thick yarn or a fine cord. Thread a double loop into a heavy needle and use this as a lever to pull the heavy yarn through.
Thread a second needle with a finer matching or contrasting yarn. Lay the thick yarn along the design line and tie it down at intervals with a short stitch taken at right angles to the design.

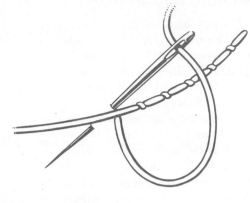

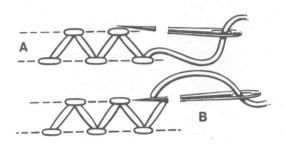

Cross stitch ▶

Complete one half of the cross at a time, first from lower right to top left and back under the fabric to lower left, and so on to the end of the line (A). Then complete the other half of the cross (B). Make sure the upper half of each stitch lies in the same direction.

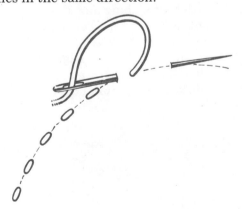

◀ Chevron stitch

Start at the lower left. Bring the needle up and make a stitch to the right. Take the needle back under and bring up half way along the stitch. Then make a stitch a little to the right on the upper line. Take a small stitch under to the left (A). Bring the needle over to make a stitch to the right and then make a small stitch under to the left to bring the needle up at the centre again (B). Work alternately on upper and lower lines.

◀ Dot stitch

Similar to running stitch in effect but of a slightly raised appearance.
Work twice over each stitch and keep the stitches small.
Work in two movements and allow the thread to lie slightly loose on the surface of the fabric.
This is a useful small stitch to break the hard edge of a large area of closely woven stitchery.

Fishbone stitch ▶

The flat stitches overlap slightly at the centre, forming a vein. The stitch can be worked as a solid line stitch, or adapted to various shapes. It is particularly useful as a filling for leaves and flower petals.

Bring the needle out at the top of the shape (A) and make a small, straight stitch. Continue down the shape, bringing the needle out at the edge (B and C) and down at the right or left of the centre as shown in the diagram.

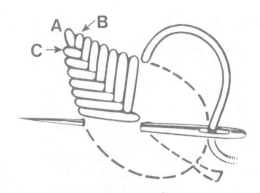

Herringbone stitch ◀

A wide line stitch, easily worked to fill a simple shape.

Bring the needle through from the back. Lay the thread diagonally and with the needle horizontal pick up a small piece of thread.

Take the needle forward again and repeat along the row.

The needle is in a horizontal position throughout the stitching.

Jacobean couching ▶

A good stitch for flower centres. Lay even threads horizontally and vertically, or diagonally. Tie down the points of intersection with small slanting stitch or cross stitch.

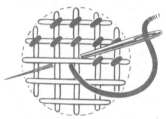

Long and short stitch ◀

Formed in the same way as satin stitch, the first row is worked with the stitches alternately long and short, following the design line. Subsequent rows are worked with stitches of equal length to retain the broken edge. Used for the blending of colours, each merges into the next in subtle tonal change.

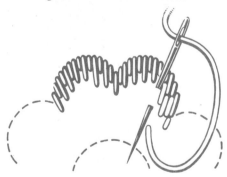

Roumanian stitch ▶

Lay a satin stitch (A) and tie it down with a slanting stitch across the centre (B). Repeat as a broad band or work it to fill a shape.

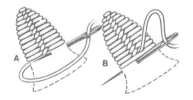

Running stitch ▶

The needle is taken in and out of an
equal length of fabric. The yarn forms a
broken line. Work it in a single line or
repeat in rows as a filling pattern.

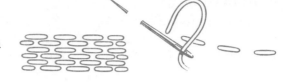

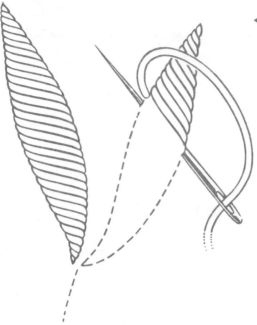

◀ Satin stitch

Simple in the working process, it needs
practice to work it well.
Straight stitches are repeated side by
side. Bring the needle up from the back
of the fabric. Take it down so that the
thread lies vertically. Bring the needle
up again beside the point at which the
yarn first came out. Repeat along the
row. Work it in a frame in two
movements. Bring the needle up from
the back, lay the thread and hold it in
position with the left forefinger. Return
the needle to the back and draw the
yarn through so that it lies lightly on
the surface of the fabric.
Use this method for all flat stitches
which need to lay smoothly side by side.

Seeding stitch ▶

An easy stitch for filling. This is made
up of small straight stitches of equal
length placed at random.

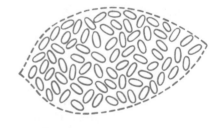

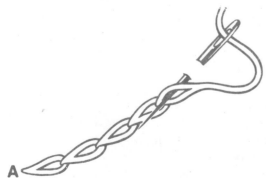

◀ Split stitch

Work as a line stitch or in rows to form
a broken surface.
Begin by bringing the needle through
at A and make a single small back
stitch on the design line, piercing the
thread with the needle.
Continue along the design line in the
same way.

Stem stitch ▶

Easy to work, this stitch is very versatile, acting as a single, fine line, a raised, or a broad line according to the method of working.

The needle comes up from the back and is put in again a little in advance of the previous stitch.

For the finest line, bring the needle up just above the previous stitch (A).

For a broader line, bring it out to one side (B).

For a raised line, work it over a laid thread.

Make the stitches smaller when following a tight curve, lengthen them on a straight line.

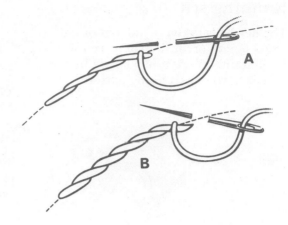

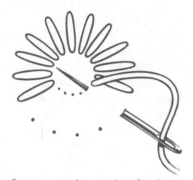

Surface satin stitch ▶

This has a slightly broken appearance and uses less wool than satin stitch as only a small amount of yarn is left at the back of the work. Lay the stitches side by side and bring the needle out again a thread or two beyond where it went in.

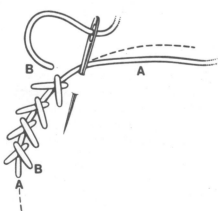

◀ Straight stitch

These stitches are single and spaced and can be used either in a regular or irregular pattern, and even or uneven in size.

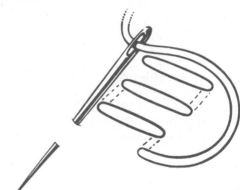

◀ Thorn stitch

A length of yarn is tied to the surface of the fabric with a decorative stitch. Bring the yarn (A) to the surface. Thread a needle with a second length of yarn (B). Work thorn-like stitches over yarn taking the needle alternately from the left and right over the laid thread.

24

LOOPED STITCHES

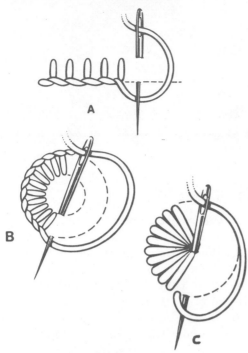

Buttonhole stitch
Open buttonhole wheel
◀ Buttonhole wheel

Buttonhole stitch is a versatile stitch to work as a single row for a neat edging, or one row below another as a filling stitch. For the latter, vary the colour in each row for an unusual colour and texture effect. Bring the needle out on the design line. Insert the needle to the right above the line, loop the thread under the needle and pull through (A). Repeat along the row, finishing with a small stitch to tie the loop. Work the stitch in a circle for the open wheels (B). Angle each stitch toward an imagined centre point.

For the Buttonhole Wheel, each stitch is taken into the centre point and a small hole is formed (C).

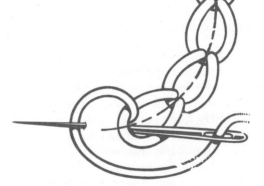

Chain stitch ▶

Bring the needle out on the design line. Put it in again next to where the yarn was brought out. Pick up a small piece of the fabric along the design line, looping the yarn under the needle. Pull the needle through, keeping the tension slack and repeat. The last stitch of a row is taken over the loop and back into the fabric to tie the loop in position. (See diagram for detached chain.)

◀ Detached buttonhole

Work a row of chain or buttonhole stitch across the shape to be filled. Work buttonhole stitch into this heading, but not into the fabric. Work alternately from left to right, then right to left. The needle is taken down into the fabric at the end of each row.

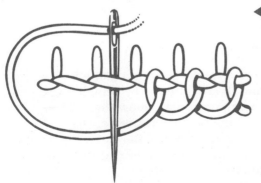

Detached chain ▶

Work it as a round stitch or with a 'tail' as for fly stitch. It makes a decorative filling either scattered freely, or in formal rows or worked in a circle. Another name is daisy stitch.

Work as for chain stitch (A), tying each stitch down as explained for finishing the row of chain stitches (B).

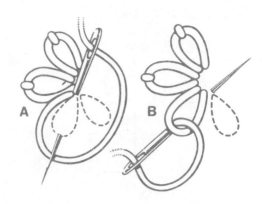

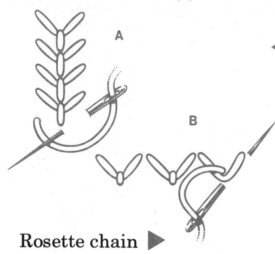

◀ Fly stitch

Work this as grouped individual stitches. Repeat one below another (A) or side by side as line stitches (B). Bring the needle out at the left of a centre line. Take it in at the opposite side and bring it out again on the centre line to form a 'Y' shape. Loop the yarn under the needle, return it at the centre line and repeat.

Rosette chain ▶

A very attractive stitch worked in two movements. Make a chain stitch over the thread coming from the right (A). Pull the yarn through so that the loop lies slightly loose on the surface of the fabric. Take the needle up under the thread (B), but not through the fabric, ready to begin the next stitch. A little practice is needed to get the scale of this stitch right. Worked too large it slips out of shape.

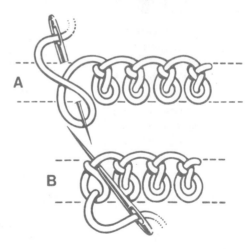

◀ Wheatear stitch

Two straight converging stitches (A and B) are followed by bringing the thread up a little below them. Then pass the needle back under the converging ends of the two stitches and back through the fabric at the same lower point (C). Repeat, with two more converging stitches (D).

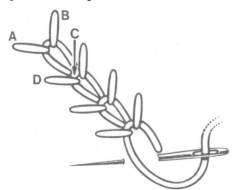

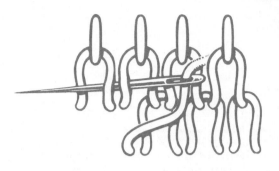

Cloud stitch

This is a useful filling stitch in which colour can be blended in a similar way to long and short stitch.

Work a row of satin stitch along the outline.

Work the second and subsequent rows by bringing the needle out below the first line. Thread the needle through the stitch immediately above and take the needle in again beside the first stitch. Take up a small piece of the fabric between each stitch and repeat along the row.

KNOT STITCHES

Coral knot ▶

This is a line stitch. The knots can be worked closely or spaced. Repeat in rows for an unusual textured surface. The needle is brought through at the right hand end of the design line. Lay the thread along the line and hold in place with the left thumb. Put the needle in just above and bring it out just below the yarn. Loop the yarn round the needle. Pull the needle and yarn through at right angles to the fabric for a well-raised knot. Repeat along the row.

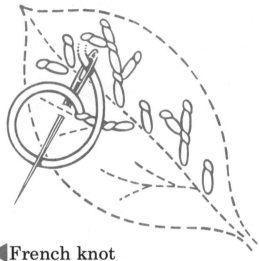

◀French knot

Work it closely or widely spaced. This is most easily worked in a frame.

To work in the hand, bring the needle through from the back. Hold a short length of yarn in position with the thumb and twist the needle under the yarn (A). Twist two or three times. Return the needle to the point next to where it came out and pull through, holding the yarn taut (B).

To work in a frame, bring the needle and yarn through. Twist the yarn round the needle once or twice with the left hand. Then return through the fabric, holding the yarn taut close to the knot and releasing it when the remaining yarn has been pulled through.

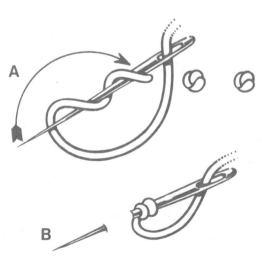

Cushions *

Oblong Cushion

Materials

2 pieces olive green embroidery linen,
20 × 16 ins for embroidery, 20 × 17 ins for
back of cushion
10 inch zipper to match fabric.
Cushion pad, 16 × 12 ins
Appleton's Crewel Wool
1 skein each of:
Bright Yellow 552, 557
Honeysuckle Yellow 693
Heraldic Gold 841
Coral 861, 865
Bright Rose Pink 942
Bright Terra Cotta 221
Orange Red 441
Mauve 604
Purple 106
Sky Blue 564, 566
Chocolate 181
Putty Grounding 998
Early English Green 542, 548
Drab Green 333
White 991
Crewel Embroidery needle, medium-size
Finished size, including edging: 18 × 14 ins

Instructions

Please note: Embroider throughout with
1 strand except when working with
Honeysuckle Yellow 693 and Coral 865,
which should be used with 3 strands.
Mark the centre of the fabric with vertical
and horizontal basting stitch. Enlarge
design to 8 inches deep and transfer to
fabric, making certain that the centre of the
pattern lines up with the centre point
marked on the fabric. Follow chart overleaf
and key for colours and stitches. When
complete, press fabric on wrong side.

Making Up

Cut back piece (20 × 17 ins) in half lengthwise and rejoin pieces by inserting zipper.
Complete seams each side of zip. (Diagram 2
overleaf). Stitch back and front sections all
round. Turn right side out and topstitch
1½ inches from edge to form a band round
the cushion.

Stitch Key

⊞ Couched down
xx Cross stitch
\\ Half-cross stitch
✗ Cross stitch with French knot in centre
▨ Crossed over laid filling
✍ Chain stitch with Fly stitch
• French knot
≡ Laidwork
▧ Laid and filled completely
✳ Laid and crossed at points
⊞ Laid thread couched down
⊞ Laid (3 strands) couched with same colour

Colour Key

1–865 Coral
2–333 Drab Green
3–548 Early English Green
4–988 Putty grounding
5–106 Purple
6–557 Bright yellow
7–552 Bright yellow
8–181 Chocolate
9–841 Heraldic Gold
10–861 Coral
11–566 Sky Blue
12–221 Bright Terra Cotta
13–441 Orange Red
14–991 White
15–564 Sky Blue
16–604 Mauve
17–942 Bright Rose Pink
18–542 Early English Green
19–693 Honeysuckle Yellow

Designed and worked by Renata Gottschalk

Materials

1 yd single thread evenweave cream linen,
28 threads to the inch, 22 ins wide
Cushion pad, 16 ins diameter
Finished size: 16 ins diameter
Appleton's Crewel Wool
1 skein each of:
Bright Yellow 551, 552, 553, 554, 555, 556, 557
Cornflower 461, 462, 463, 464
Crewel Embroidery needle, medium-size

Instructions

Cut out two circles of fabric, each to 18
inches diameter. Work on one piece. Half
the design is given. Enlarge, reversing
design for other half, to 10¼ inches diameter.
Trace onto fabric. Follow chart and key for
colours and stitches. Work throughout
with one strand. When complete, press on
wrong side.

Making Up

On both pieces, turn edges in 1 inch and
baste. Use open buttonhole stitch to secure
edges. On both pieces of the cushion, inside
the edging, embroider a decorative row of
whipped chain stitch. Using 3 long strands
of 552, join back and front together by
threading through the loops of the open
buttonhole stitch, leaving enough open to
slip in cushion. Close up remainder. Knot
the ends of the strands together. Slip
strands inside cushion. This method will
enable you to undo part of the cushion
cover quite easily for laundering or dry
cleaning.

Stitch Key

OO Chain stitch
⁜ Split stitch
≡ Closed buttonhole
⋀ Straight stitch
⊞ 3 strands laid and couched
⋯ Weaving (pick up every 4th thread alternate)
⋙ Stem stitch

Colour Key

1–551 Bright Yellow
2–552 Bright Yellow
3–553 Bright Yellow
4–554 Bright Yellow
5–555 Bright Yellow
6–556 Bright Yellow
7–557 Bright Yellow
8–461 Cornflower
9–462 Cornflower
10–463 Cornflower
11–464 Cornflower

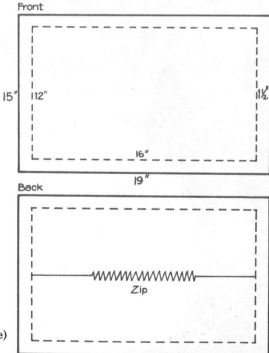

Diagram 1. Putting the zip into cushion

30

Diagram 1. Pattern stitch and colour key for oblong cushion. Enlarge to 8ins deep

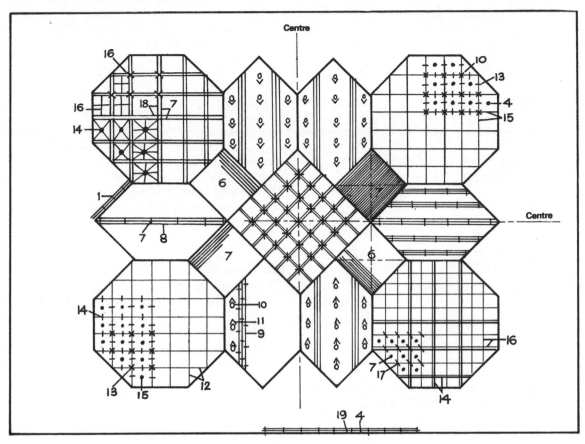

Diagram 3. Half of round cushion pattern. Reverse for second half, enlarge the whole motif to 10¼ins diameter

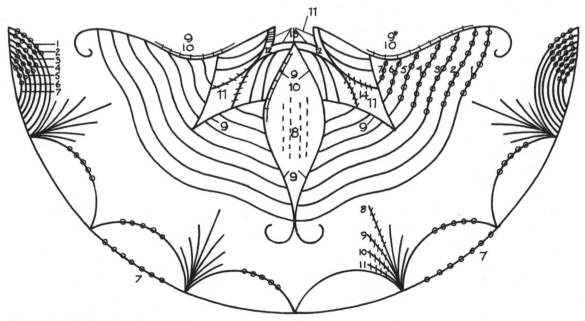

31

Doll Pyjama Case *

Materials

Patterned cotton, ¼ yd × 36 ins wide
Plain cotton, ¾ yd × 36 ins wide
13 inch zipper
Kapok
Appleton's Crewel Wool
1 skein each of:
Leaf Green 425
Signal Green 436
Lime 997
White 991
Cornflower 465
Finished size: 22 ins high

Instructions

Draw out the patterns which are given
overleaf and cut out all the pieces, allowing
¼ in seam allowance. Transfer the designs
to front of the bag and the face markings to
the front of the head. Follow the chart and
key for stitches and colours, using 2 strands
for the stem stitch outlines and for the
herringbone stitch flower border and 1
strand for the remainder. Press on wrong
side.

Making Up

Cut the back section of the skirt-bag at the
centre line and insert the zip.
Baste bag front and back, right sides
together and stitch leaving top open.
Turn to the right side.
Hem the front edges of the cape and tack
the sides in position to the sides of the bag.
Cut 8 strands of Lime 997 for hair and
attach to the front of the head. Fold
the strap lengthwise and stitch. Turn to
the right side and press.
With right sides together, join the back and
front of the head, leaving the neck open and
1½ inches at the top of the head. Turn to
right side, press and stuff lightly with

kapok. Slip the strap ends in and stitch to
secure. Pleat up the top of the bag to fit the
neck edge. Turn in and overlap the neck
edge. Stitch the head to the bag with two
rows of stitching for added strength. Finish
by tying the ribbon at the neck.

Stitch Key

ɰ Buttonhole
⊛ Buttonhole wheel
⊕ Open buttonhole wheel
Ϙϙ Detached chain
⠿ Dot stitch
Y Y Fly stitch
XXX Herringbone
//// Stem stitch

Colour Key

1–425 Leaf Green
2–436 Signal Green
3–997 Lime
4–991 White
5–465 Cornflower

Doll's face markings for head piece

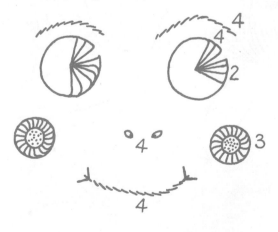

Designed and worked by Elizabeth Manley

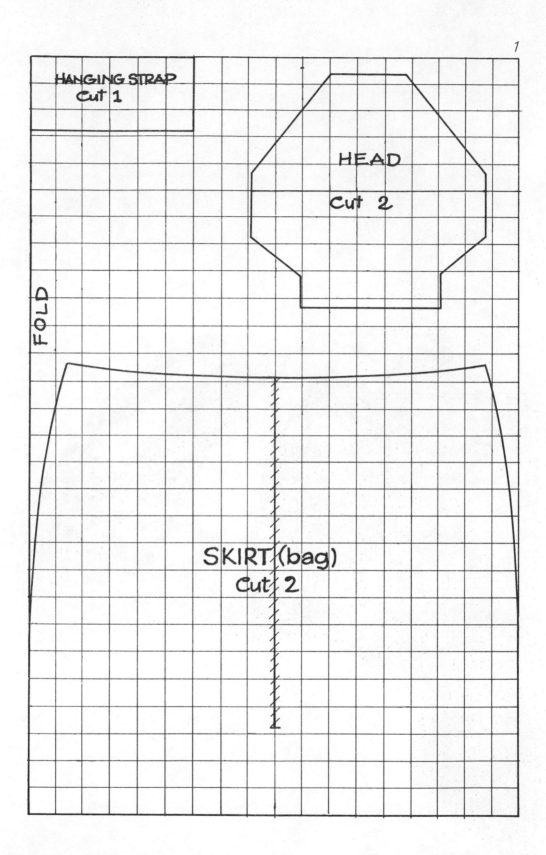

HANGING STRAP
Cut 1

HEAD
Cut 2

FOLD

SKIRT (bag)
Cut 2

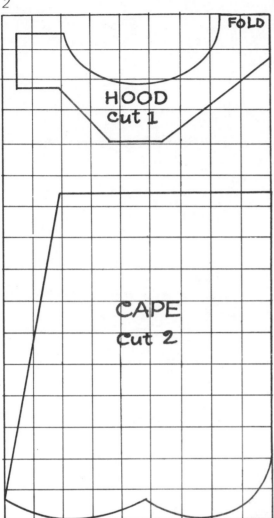

2

FOLD

HOOD
cut 1

CAPE
Cut 2

Diagrams 1, 2. Graph patterns for Doll
Pyjama case: 1 sq=1 inch

Diagram 3. Three designs for front of bag
Enlarge pattern to 6 ins wide

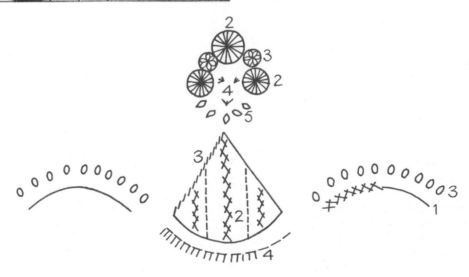

Curtain Border *

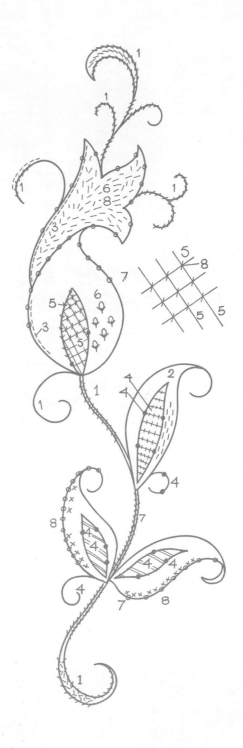

Materials

½ yd × 50 ins wide natural coloured linen
or medium weight curtain material (or
desired yardage and width to fit your
window)
Curtain rings or other fittings of choice
Matching sewing thread
Appleton's Crewel Wool:
1 skein each of:
Chocolate 187
Peacock Blue 642, 644, 645, 646
Honeysuckle Yellow 693, 695, 697
Crewel Embroidery needle

Instructions

Enlarge the design and then transfer it
to material. Place design 6½ ins away from
lower edge of material and repeat with
1 in apart. Embroider with 1 strand
throughout. Follow chart and key for
colours and stitches. Press on wrong side.

Making Up

Turn hem along both sides and bottom and
slip stitch. Finish top of curtain according
to choice of fittings.

Stitch Key

   Chain stitch with Fly stitch
   Couching
   Jacobean couching
   Seed stitch
   Stem stitch

Colour Key

1–187 Chocolate
2–642 Peacock Blue
3–644 Peacock Blue
4–645 Peacock Blue
5–646 Peacock Blue
6–693 Honeysuckle Yellow
7–695 Honeysuckle Yellow
8–697 Honeysuckle Yellow

Designed and worked by Renata Gottschalk.

Hand Bag

Illustrated on page 4

Materials

1st Working
½ yd × 36 ins wide of medium weight linen
for surface embroidery, in orange
½ yd × 36 ins wide of cotton for lining in
matching colour
Matching sewing threads
1 pair of cane handles
Round frame
Finished size: 13 × 16 ins plus handles
Appelton's Crewel Wool
1 skein each of:
Chocolate 187
Early English Green 542, 544, 546
Bright Yellow 552, 553, 556
Putty Grounding 989
Crewel Embroidery needle, medium-size

2nd Working
Appleton's Crewel Wool
1 skein each of:
Drab Green 338
Bright Yellow 553, 557
Putty Grounding 989
Peacock Blue 642, 645
Crewel Embroidery needle, medium-size

Instructions

Cut out 2 pieces each from both the
embroidery fabric and lining 15 × 18 ins.
Find the horizontal centre on each piece of
the embroidery fabric and mark with basting
stitches. Enlarge design and place design
3 ins away from lower edge of fabric,
making sure that the centre of the design
lines up with the centre of the fabric.
Transfer design to fabric. Follow chart and
key for colour and stitches, work both sides
of the bag. Press embroidery on wrong side.

Making Up

Place both pieces right sides together and
tack and stitch the bottom of the bag
taking 1 in seam. Tack and stitch sides
together leaving 5 ins opening at top
of each side. Press seams and turn right
side out. Sew lining in the same way, but do
not turn right side out, press seams and slip
into inside of bag.

Trim top of lining to correspond with top of
bag, turn raw edges in and slip stitch
together. Pull top edge through handle and
stitch top edge to lining just below the
handles. Stitch material and lining together
just below the handles across the bag.

Stitch Key   1st Working

✕✕ Cross stitch
ᓇᓇ Detached chain stitch
    between 2 straight stitches
    (Tete-de-boeuf filling)
ᵛᵛ Fly stitch with French knots
《《 Raised Fishbone stitch
╫╫ Stem stitch (1 row)
•• Stem stitch (2 rows)

Colour Key

1–187 Chocolate
2–542 Early English Green
3–544 Early English Green
4–546 Early English Green
5–552 Bright Yellow
6–553 Bright Yellow
7–556 Bright Yellow
8–989 Putty Grounding

Stitch Key   2nd Working

∞ Chain stitch
∞∞ Chain stitch (solid filling)
ᵧᵧ Wheatear
✷ Laidwork couched down
◩ Satin stitch
⁝⁝⁝ Seed stitch
╫╫ Stem stitch

Colour Key

1–338 Drab Green
2–553 Bright Yellow
3–557 Bright Yellow
4–989 Putty Grounding
5–642 Peacock Blue
6–645 Peacock Blue

Designed and worked by Renata Gottschalk.

Top: stitch and colour key for 1st working
Centre: Detail of 1st working
Bottom: Stitch and colour key for 2nd working.

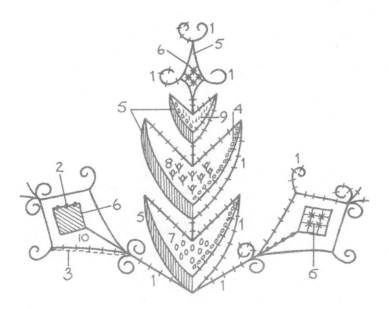

39

Upholstered Stool Cover

Materials

Blue Hessian, approximately 18 threads to an inch, 46 ins long × 25 ins wide
Final size: 36 × 15 ins with an extra inch worked for upholstery purposes
Appleton's Crewel Wool
10 skeins each of:
Off-white 992
Sky Blue 561, 563, 564, 565, 566, 568
2 skeins Bright Yellow 557
Tapestry needle

Instructions

First of all, mark the centre of the fabric with vertical and horizontal basting stitches. Begin work at centre (with Bright Yellow 557) and follow chart overleaf and key for colour.
Work with 2 strands throughout over 4 threads, using straight stitches (Florentine stitches diagram, page 43).

Making Up

The upholstery of stool shown was done by a professional upholsterer.

Stitch Key

‖ Straight stitch throughout

Colour Key

1–568 Sky Blue
2–566 Sky Blue
3–565 Sky Blue
4–564 Sky Blue
5–563 Sky Blue
6–561 Sky Blue
7–992 Off White
8–557 Bright Yellow

Designed and worked by Renata Gottschalk
Stool designed and upholstered by Ridwan Dobson

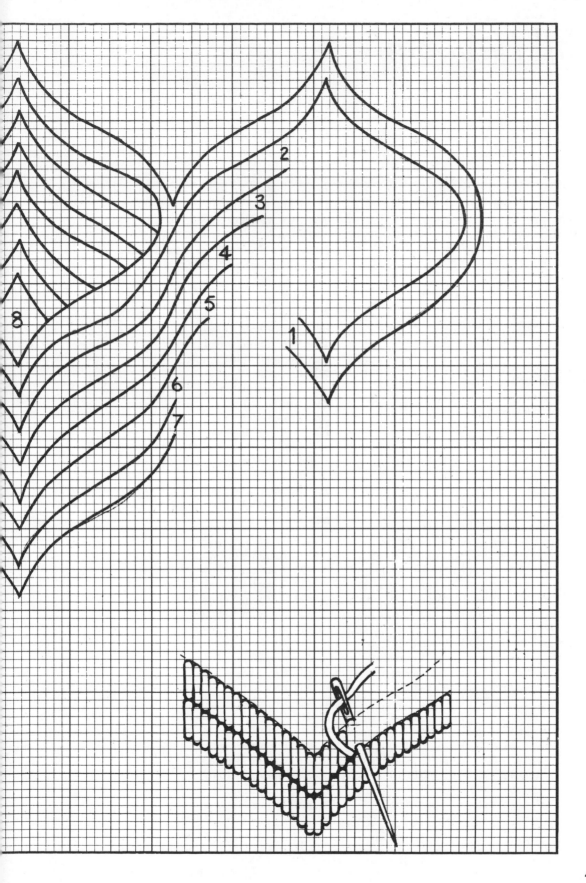

Wall Hanging *

Materials

Brown linen, 30 × 20 ins
Curtain pole
Finished size: 25 × 15 ins
Appleton's Crewel Wool
1 skein each of:
Bright Yellow 552
Autumn Yellow 472, 473, 474, 476, 479
Brown Olive 311
Sky Blue 562, 565, 567
Cornflower 461, 462, 463
Olive Green 244
Bright Mauve 453
2 skeins each of:
Heraldic Gold 844
Early English Green 542
3 skeins of:
Honeysuckle Yellow 696
Ring frame

Instructions

First find the centre of the linen fabric
by basting horizontal and vertical lines.
Enlarge the design to 11 ins wide and
transfer to the fabric. Follow the chart
overleaf and stitch and colour keys. Use 2
strands to outline the star. Work a second
row with a single strand. 2 strands are used
for the buttonhole wheel at the centre and a
single strand for the long chain stitches
worked over it.
Use 2 strands for the bird's head, 2 strands
for the wide flower petals. Vary number of
strands throughout for textural interest.
When complete, press on wrong side.

Making Up

Machine stitch both sides about ½ in in from
the edge and fringe. At the top, make a
casing to fit the curtain pole. Hand stitch so
that the stitches do not show at the front.
Turn a narrow hem at the lower edge.
Cut 7-in lengths of colour 696 and small

amounts of 479 and 476. Take 10 threads at
a time and fold in half. Pull through the
hem edge with a crochet hook and knot
into a tassle. *illustrated overleaf*
Appleton's Crewel Wool is used single
throughout unless double thread is
indicated – (d)

Stitch Key

m   Buttonhole (stitches close together)
ᵾᵾᵾ Buttonhole filling
⊗   Buttonhole wheel
ᴜᴜ Detached buttonhole
ᵚᵚ Chain stitch
oo Couched stitch
ɤɤ Cretan stitch
66 French knot
XX Herringbone stitch
+++ Laid and couched (Oriental stitch)
|·|·| Long and short stitch
mr Rosette chain
⇌   Roumanian stitch
///// Satin stitch
ᴅᴅᴅ Square chain

Colour Key

1–552 Bright Yellow
2–472 Autumn Yellow
3–473 Autumn Yellow
4–474 Autumn Yellow
5–476 Autumn Yellow
6–479 Autumn Yellow
7–311 Brown Olive
8–562 Sky Blue
9–565 Sky Blue
10–567 Sky Blue
11–461 Cornflower
12–462 Cornflower
13–463 Cornflower
14–244 Olive Green
15–453 Bright Mauve
16–844 Heraldic Gold
17–542 Early English Green
18–696 Honeysuckle Yellow

Designed and worked by Lydia Cole-Powney

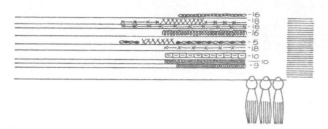

Diagram 1. Stages of making a tassel
Diagram 2. Stitch diagram and colour key for the border at the bottom of the wall hanging

2

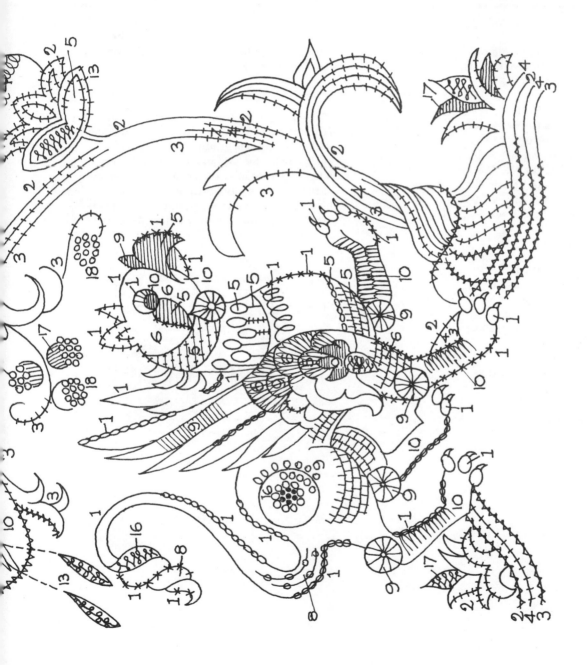

Placemats

Materials

(for each placemat)
Single thread cream evenweave linen,
28 threads to the inch, $20 \times 15\frac{1}{2}$ ins
Final size: $18 \times 13\frac{1}{2}$ ins

Placemat No 1
Appleton's Crewel Wool
1 skein each of:
Golden Brown 903, 904
Bright Yellow 552, 556
Honeysuckle Yellow 694
Bright Rose Pink 942, 945
Early English Green 542, 544
Sky Blue 568
Mauve 604

Placemat No 2
Appleton's Crewel Wool
1 skein each of:
Golden Brown 905
Honeysuckle Yellow 694
Bright Yellow 552
Coral 861
Early English Green 554
Sky Blue 563
Mauve 604
Bright Rose Pink 942, 945
Mauve 602

Instructions

Enlarge the design and trace it onto the
fabric. Embroider with 1 strand, following
chart overleaf. Press on wrong side.

Making Up

Measure $1\frac{3}{4}$ins in from edge of fabric. Cut
fabric threads at the centre of each side and
withdraw threads gradually outwards on
each side to the corners, leaving sufficient
lengths of thread at the corners in order to
darn the ends away invisibly. Turn back
hem to the drawn threads, mitre the corners
and baste. Hemstitch over 3 threads of the
fabric, using Antique Hemstitch.

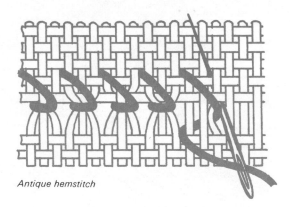

Antique hemstitch

Designed and worked by Renata Gottschalk

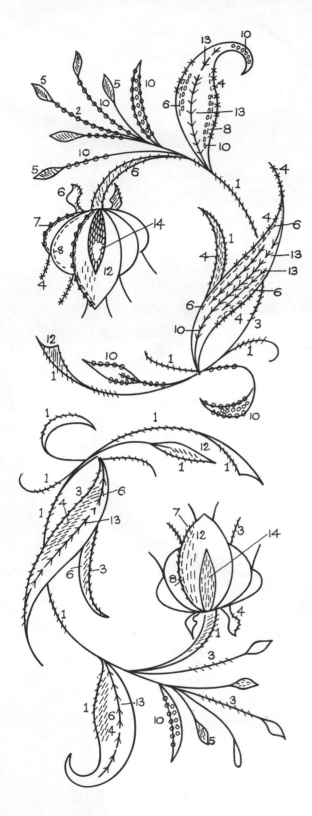

Stitch Key

✗✗ Cross stitch
↞↞ Fly stitch
•• French knot
✳✳ Open fishbone stitch
//// Satin stitch
⸭⸭⸭ Seed stitch
ΦΦ Split stitch
ⱶⱶⱶ Stem stitch
/— Straight stitch

Colour Key

1–903 Golden Brown
2–904 Golden Brown
3–905 Golden Brown
4–552 Bright Yellow
5–556 Bright Yellow
6–694 Honeysuckle Yellow
7–942 Bright Rose Pink
8–945 Bright Rose Pink
9–542 Early English Green
10–544 Early English Green
11–568 Sky Blue
12–563 Sky Blue
13–861 Coral
14–604 Mauve
15–602 Mauve

Pattern for Placemat No 1

50

Pattern for Placemat No 2

51

Long Skirt

Materials

36 in wide fine wool, dress weight;
size 12, approximately 4 yds.
Lining fabric to same quantity
Matching threads
Black mull for backing embroidery
8-in skirt zip
Hooks and eyes
Rectangular floor frame, size 30 ins tape
Appleton's Crewel Wool
3 skeins each of:
Chocolate 181, 183
Early English Green 541
Honeysuckle Yellow 693
2 skeins of:
Peacock Blue 642
Crewel needle, medium-size

Instructions

Begin by drawing out a paper pattern
from the graph pattern. (The skirt has four
panels, the seams running on the front and
back but not on the hip line. The zip is
inserted into the seam left back.) Transfer
the outline of the pattern pieces to the
fabric. Enlarge design to 20 ins deep, and
transfer to fabric once on each panel. Place
mull in frame, securing it tightly. Place
traced fabric onto mull, stretching it
slightly in order to avoid fabric puckering
when removing from frame. Pin edges down.
At 6-in intervals, baste both horizontally
and vertically over the entire panel.
Embroider with 1 strand throughout in
stem stitch, except for the flower heads,
which are worked in seed stitch. Follow
chart overleaf and key for colours and
stitches. Press on wrong side.

Making Up

Sew panels together. Make up the waistband. Insert 8-in zip into right back seam.
Attach waistband and sew on hooks and
eyes. Take up hem. Make up lining as for
skirt but without waistband. Slipstitch
lining to the inside skirt waist.

Graph pattern for skirt:
Extend dotted lines for skirt length

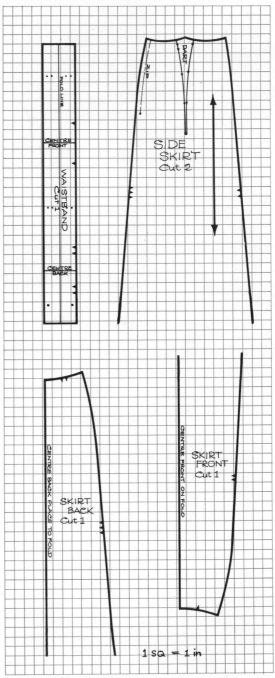

Designed and worked by Renata Gottschalk

Stitch Key

🌀 Stem stitch
— Seeding stitch

Colour Key

1–183 Chocolate
2–693 Honeysuckle Yellow
3–642 Peacock Blue
4–541 Early English Green
5–181 Chocolate

*Enlarge this design to 20 ins deep for
each of the four skirt panels*

54

55

Pocket Tidy for Child's Room *

Materials

1¼ yds cream-coloured curtain fabric, 48 ins wide

Heavy-weight iron-on interlining for pockets and backing

Supporting pole or rod

Ring frame

Appleton's Crewel Wool

2 skeins each of:

Sea Green 401

Bright Rose Pink 944

Off-white 992

1 skein each of:

Leaf Green 427

Cornflower 464

Early English Green 543

Bright Yellow 552, 554

Sky Blue 564

Mauve 604

Honeysuckle Yellow 698

Coral 862

Bright Rose Pink 946

Instructions

Cut three strips from the width of the fabric 7½ ins deep. Measure out each strip for pockets (Diagram 1), and transfer the enlarged designs to the fabric in the areas indicated. Follow the chart overleaf and key for stitches and colours. Press on wrong side.

Appleton's Crewel Wool is used single throughout unless double thread is indicated – (d)

Making Up

Back each of the pocket strips with iron-on interlining fabric. Make a 1-in hem on the top edge and top-stitch on the fold. Turn a ½-in hem along the bottom edge and press. Cut the backing for the tidy in two pieces each 20 ins × 13½ ins. Seam to make a piece 26 ins deep × 20 ins. Back the fabric with iron-on interlining.

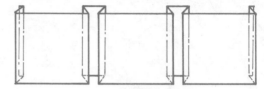

Diagram 2. Fold pocket sections as shown

Pleat the pocket strips with the fingers and pin as shown in diagram 2. Press and then pin and baste the pockets to the backing piece. Stitch across the bottom of each pocket strip and then down the sides. Work a single row of machine stitches between first, second and third pockets, stitching from top to bottom. Work loop ties between each pocket to hold the shape.

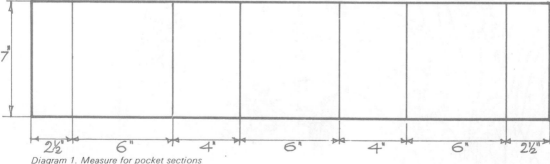

Diagram 1. Measure for pocket sections

Designed and worked by Lydia Cole-Powney

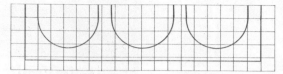

Diagram 3. Draw scooped top to 20 ins wide

To make the scooped heading, cut a strip of fabric 7½ ins deep by 20 ins wide. Draw out a pattern for the heading (Diagram 3), and draw it onto the wrong side of the strip. Pin and baste the strip to the top edge of the tidy and machine stitch along the pattern lines, outlining the scoops. Cut out the scoops, ¼ in from the stitching, clip into curves, turn to right side and press. Neaten the ends of the straps and stitch firmly to the back of the panel. Turn in the long sides of the tidy and stitch. Turn a hem at the bottom and top stitch. The hanging rod slips through the straps.

Making Up

Appleton's Crewel Wool is used single throughout unless double thread is indicated – (d)

Stitch Key

ᵾᵾᵾ	Buttonhole stitch
⊛	Buttonhole wheel
ᵾᵾᵾ	Detached buttonhole
∞	Chain stitch
++	Cross stitch
OO	Single couching stitch
♂♂	Detached chain
✗✗	Cretan stitch
⊙⊙	French knots
XX	Herringbone stitch
≣	Satin stitch

Colour Key

1–401 Sea Green
2–944 Bright Rose Pink
3–992 Off-White
4–427 Leaf Green
5–464 Cornflower
6–543 Early English Green
7–552 Bright Yellow
8–554 Bright Yellow
9–564 Sky Blue
10–604 Mauve
11–698 Honeysuckle
12–862 Coral
13–946 Bright Rose Pink

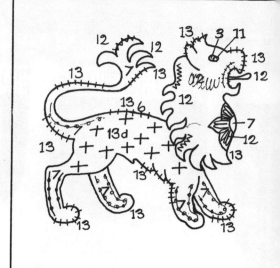

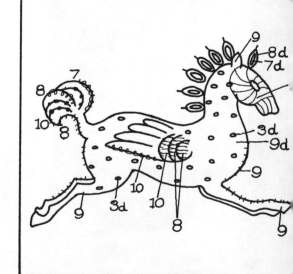

Jewel Box

Materials

$\frac{1}{4}$ yd of 36 ins wide cream linen
Finished size: $4\frac{1}{2}$ ins in diameter $\times$ $2\frac{1}{2}$ ins deep
$\frac{1}{4}$ yd navy blue lining, 36 ins wide
$\frac{1}{3}$ yd wadding (acetate, rayon, etc.)
15 ins narrow elastic
Navy and cream sewing thread
Stiff card 9×25 ins
Sellotape
Ring frame
Appleton's Crewel Wool
1 skein each of:
Leaf Green 422, 425
Fuchsia 805
Cornflower 463, 465

Instructions

Cut out a square 9×9 ins, from the cream linen. Mark the centre horizontally and vertically with basting stitches. Trace the design onto tissue paper, including the outer circle. Baste to the centre of the square, then transfer the design onto the fabric. Using 1 strand throughout, follow the chart and key overleaf for colours and stitches. Press on wrong side.

Making Up

Make the base of the box first.
Cut a piece of card about $14 \times 2\frac{1}{2}$ ins. Butt the short ends together and secure with small pieces of Sellotape. Cover with wadding. Cut a strip of linen 15×4 ins, as shown on the cutting layout below – Diagram 1. Stitch into a circle so that it fits smoothly over the card and wadding. Turn the seam allowance over the card and secure with long herringbone stitches taken from the top to the bottom of the fabric. Pad the inside. Make the lining for this section, cutting as for the outer fabric. Cut the second strip of fabric, about $1\frac{1}{2} \times 15$ ins for the pockets.
Turn in a narrow hem and thread in the elastic so that the top is slightly gathered. Turn in the seam allowance on the lining and the pockets and slip stitch to the lower edge of the side. Stitch the pocket inside the box so that it is divided into four sections. Cut a $4\frac{1}{2}$ ins circle of card for the base. Cut a circle of linen $5\frac{1}{2}$ ins in diameter. Lay the card on the linen and fold the seam allowance over the card. Fix in place with long stitches as shown (Diagram 2). Stab stitch the sides to the base.
Cut a circle of card, slightly smaller than the base. Pad with wadding and cover with navy blue lining fabric. Gently push into position inside the box.
To make the lid, cut a strip of card for the rim (about $14\frac{1}{2} \times \frac{1}{2}$ ins). Cut linen $15 \times 1\frac{1}{2}$ ins. Join the circle of card as for the sides.

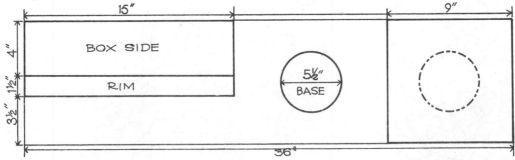

Diagram 1.

Designed by Margaret Beautement, worked by Elizabeth Manley

Make sure it will fit easily over the box
sides allowing extra for the thickness of
the linen.
Cover with the joined linen and oversew the
edges together. Make the top as for the
base, lightly padding with wadding.
Stab stitch top and rim together.
Make a lining for the lid as for the base.
Push into place, first securing the centre
with a little glue. The seams of fabric boxes
can also be joined together with Cretan
stitch. This gives a strong, decorative
edging, particularly when worked in a
contrasting coloured thread (Diagram 4).

Stitch Key

⊛   Buttonhole wheel
◓◓   French knot
≡   Satin stitch
/////   Stem stitch

Colour Key

1–422 Leaf Green
2–425 Leaf Green
3–805 Fuchsia
4–463 Cornflower
5–465 Cornflower

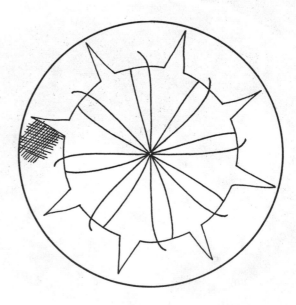

Diagram 2. Lacing the fabric

62

Diagram 3. Same-size design for
jewel box top

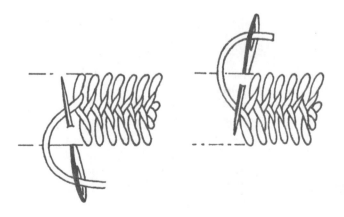

Diagram 4. Cretan stitch

63

Three Small Pictures *

Materials

Ochre yellow cotton, $\frac{3}{8}$ yd $\times$ 36 ins wide
Green cotton, $\frac{1}{2}$ yd $\times$ 36 ins wide
Strawboard, 4 pieces
1 – 22 $\times$ 9 ins
1 – $9\frac{1}{4}$ $\times$ $6\frac{1}{4}$ ins
2 – $4\frac{1}{2}$ $\times$ $6\frac{1}{4}$ ins
Final sizes: Butterfly picture $9\frac{1}{4}$ $\times$ $6\frac{1}{4}$ ins
Insects and flowers $4\frac{1}{2}$ $\times$ $6\frac{1}{4}$ ins
Complete mount   22 $\times$ 9 ins
Fabric adhesive
Ring frame
Appleton's Crewel Wool
1 skein each of:
Brown Grounding 588
Bright Yellow 554
Honeysuckle Yellow 697
Cornflower 463
Signal Green 438
Leaf Green 423
Grass Green 253
Sky Blue 568
Bright Rose Pink 945, 947
Purple 106
Bright Mauve 456
White 992

Instructions

Start by embroidering the three pictures
before cutting. Baste outlines for the picture
areas, allowing 2 ins margin around each
one. Baste vertical and horizontal lines to
mark the centres. Transfer design to fabric.
(Make sure that the insects face in opposite
directions.)

Butterfly
Follow the chart, beginning at the highest
point, using 2 strands. For the laid work on
the upper wing, use single strand. Use
2 strands for the body (herringbone stitch).
Leaves on the right are worked with
2 strands; those on the left with 1. After

completing chain stitch in white, thread
Honeysuckle Yellow 697 through tapestry
needle and stitch over and under each chain
without taking the yarn through the fabric.

Insects and flowers
Work throughout with 1 strand, following
the chart and key for colours and stitches.
Press on wrong side.

Making Up

Cover the 22 $\times$ 9 ins board with the green
cotton. Follow the directions on page 71 for
mounting the Frieze for the Child's Room.
Cut out each picture, keeping a margin of at
least 1 inch all round. Mount onto the
three small boards.
Mark the centre of the large board and the
centre of the butterfly picture with pins.
Match the centres and glue in position.
Glue the two small pictures leaving about
$\frac{1}{2}$ in between each picture.

*Designed by Margaret Beautement, worked by
Frances Doe and the Dorothy Kendall Group*

Stitch Key

- ⬭⬭⬭ Chain stitch
- •─•─• Coral knot
- ◖◗ Detached chain
- ⋰⋱ Dot stitch
- ◕◔ French knot
- ⚜ Fishbone stitch
- ⚟ Laid work stitches
- ⹀⹀ Long and short stitch
- ✕✕ Herringbone stitch
- - - - Running stitch
- //// Stem stitch

Colour Key

1–588 Brown Grounding
2–554 Bright Yellow
3–568 Sky Blue
4–463 Cornflower
5–438 Signal Green
6–423 Leaf Green
7–697 Honeysuckle Yellow
8–945 Bright Rose Pink
9–947 Bright Rose Pink
10–106 Purple
11–456 Bright Mauve
12–253 Grass Green
13–992 White

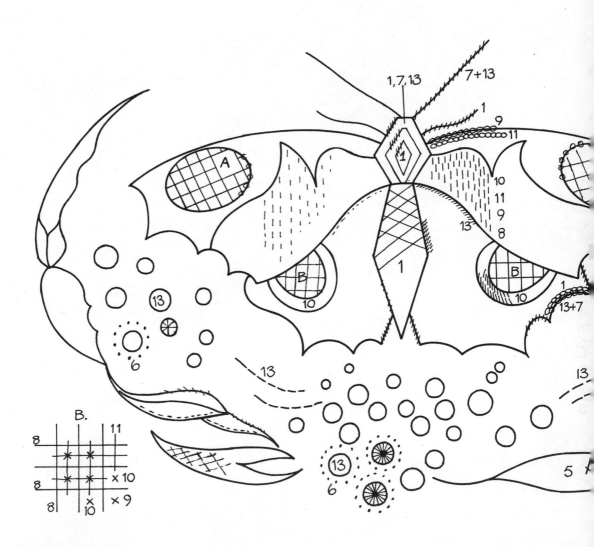

66

Bottom left: Design for Butterfly picture
Right: Insects and flowers: make sure that
the insects face in opposite directions

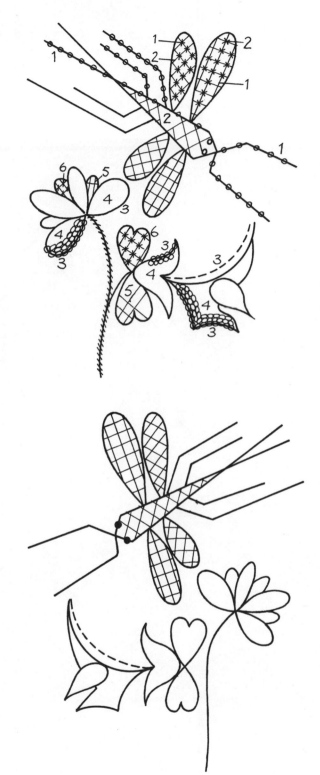

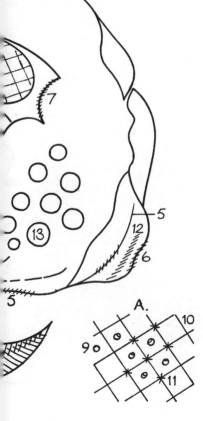

Frieze for a Child's Room *

as illustrated on preceding page

Materials

Linen and synthetic-fibre mixture fabric in
brown, 18 × 36 ins
Ring frame
Hardboard 26 × 10½ ins
Adhesive
Self-adhesive wall mounts
Appleton's Crewel Wool
1 skein each of:
Bright Rose Pink 946
Fuchsia 801, 805
Scarlet 505
Cornflower 463, 464, 465
Bright Yellow 554
Grass Green 254
Early English Green 548

Instructions

First of all, enlarge the design. With
running stitch, outline the 26 × 10½ ins area
for the embroidery, allowing a margin all
around. Run the stitches along the thread
of the fabric. (The straight line will help
when mounting the embroidery.)
Transfer design to fabric.
Mount the deer at the left into the ring
frame and stitch the laid work filling.
Outline the area with herringbone stitch.
As indicated, stitch a circlet of detached
chain over the laid work. Remove from the
frame. All the outlines are worked in stem
stitch. Use 3 strands for a bold effect for the
deer, 2 for the remaining outlines.
Follow the stitch and colour suggestions on
the chart. Work the outlines first and fit
towards the centre. Press on wrong side.

*Designed by Margaret Beautement, worked by the
Dorothy Kendall Group*

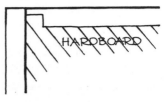

*When mounting fabric on hard-
board, glue down two sides and
trim corners as shown.*

Making Up

Lay the embroidery face down onto a fabric
pad. Match the hardboard to the running
stitch outline, making sure that the threads
of the fabric lie parallel to the edge of the
board. Apply the adhesive along one long
edge of the board. Fold the fabric allowance
over and press firmly in position. Trim the
excess fabric. Repeat for the opposite long
side, making sure that the embroidery is
fully stretched on the board. Trim at the
corners as shown in the diagram above right
and stick the remaining two sides in
position.
Fasten to the wall with self adhesive mounts.

Stitch Key

- Buttonhole stitch
- Chain stitch
- Coral knot
- Detached chain
- Detached chain wheel
- Herringbone stitch
- Laid work tied with small crosses
- Open buttonhole wheel
- Open long and short stitch
- Running stitch
- Stem stitch
- Straight stitch

Colour Key

1–946 Bright Rose Pink
2–801 Fuchsia
3–805 Fuchsia
4–505 Scarlet
5–463 Cornflower
6–464 Cornflower
7–465 Cornflower
8–554 Bright Yellow
9–254 Grass Green
10–548 Early English Green

71

Belt

Materials

Slub weave light brown linen, 30 × 9 ins
Non-woven interlining, 30 × 2 ins
Lining fabric, 30 × 6 ins
Belt buckle
Finished size: For 26-in waist
Appleton's Crewel Wool
1 skein each of:
Autumn Yellow 476, 477, 479
Bright Yellow 551, 556

From the brown slub weave linen fabric,
cut a strip 30 × 5½ ins. Oversew the edge to
prevent the fabric fraying. With running
stitch, mark the centre line down the length
of the fabric. Transfer design to fabric,
matching the centre lines. Follow the charts
overleaf and stitch and colour keys, using
3 strands for the chain stitch and stem
stitch in Autumn Yellow 479 and 2 strands
for the second row of stem stitch in Bright
Yellow 556. Press on wrong side.

Making Up

Tack the interlining to the centre on the
wrong side. Trim seams to ½ in on the long
sides. Herringbone the seam allowance to
the interlining (Diagram 1). Turn in the
seam allowance on the lining for the belt
and trim excess fabric. Slip stitch to back of
belt (Diagram 2). Adjust to waist size and
thread the ends into the buckle links.
Stitch firmly in position.

Stitch Key

Chain stitch
Stem stitch

Colour Key

1–479 Autumn Yellow
2–477 Autumn Yellow
3–476 Autumn Yellow
4–556 Bright Yellow
5–551 Bright Yellow

interlining

Diagram 1. Herringbone seam allowance to
interlining.
Diagram 2. Slip stitch lining to belt

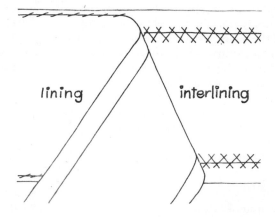

lining   interlining

Designed by Margaret Beautement, worked by
Mary Blanchard

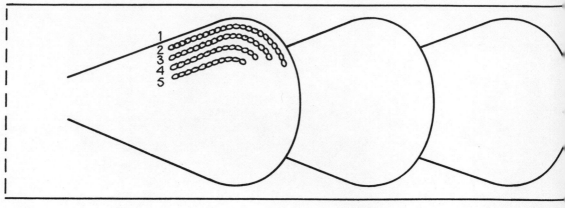

Diagram 3. Centre back motifs for belt

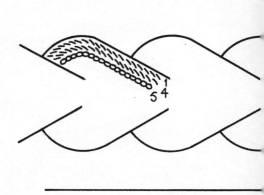

Diagram 5. Right hand end of belt, join
up with Diagram 3 left.

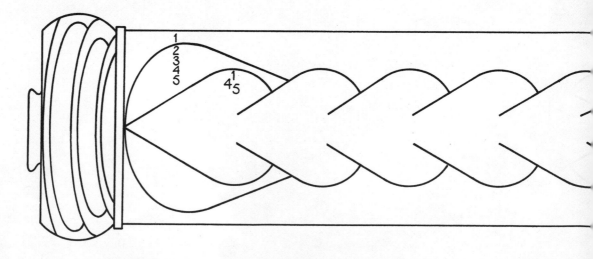

74

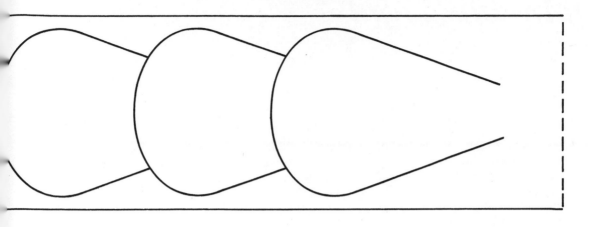

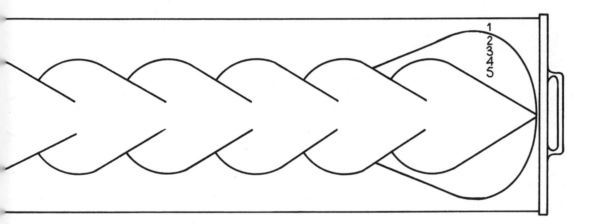

Diagram 4. Left hand end of belt, join up with diagram 3 right ▼

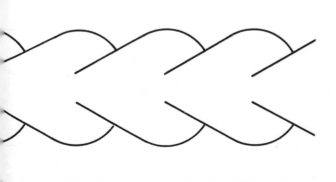

Umbrella Stand *

Try smartening up an old umbrella stand with this colourful embroidery panel. We have taken one about 8½ ins diameter and about 26–28 ins tall. You will have to measure up your own stand and buy your background material to fit.

Materials

Turquoise slubbed linen and cotton, 28 × 28 ins
Braid for trimming, 2½ yds
Fabric adhesive
Drum-shaped umbrella stand
Appleton's Crewel Wool
1 skein each of:
Mid-blue 159
Sky Blue 563, 566, 568
Bright Rose Pink 944, 947
Bright Yellow 551, 553
Peacock Blue 831
Charcoal 998
Leaf Green 426

Instructions

First of all find the centre of the fabric and mark with vertical and horizontal basting stitches. Oversew the edges to prevent fraying. Enlarge the design and transfer to centre of fabric. Use 2 strands throughout, except for Sky Blue 566, which should be used with 4 strands to work the large crosses over alternate squares. Follow the chart overleaf and key for colours and stitches. Press on wrong side.

Making Up

Turn the embroidery face down and spot fabric adhesive down one of the long edges. Turn the stand over on its side and press the fabric firmly in place, making sure that the edge is straight. Apply the adhesive to the surface of the stand and press fabric into

position. Cut the braid to fit top, bottom and the join down the length of the drum (Diagram 1). Allow ½ in for neatening at the ends. Fold over the ends and secure with a small spot of adhesive. Lightly dot the join and the top and bottom of the embroidery, and press the braid in position. Glue the length first, then the base and finally the top.

Stitch Key

- Coral knot
- Fishbone stitch
- Roumanian stitch
- Running stitch
- Stem stitch
- Laid work – see detail

Colour Key

1–159 Mid-blue
2–563 Sky Blue
3–566 Sky Blue
4–568 Sky Blue
5–944 Bright Rose Pink
6–947 Bright Rose Pink
7–551 Bright Yellow
8–553 Bright Yellow
9–831 Peacock Blue
10–998 Charcoal
11–426 Leaf Green

Designed by Margaret Beautement, worked by the Dorothy Kendall Group

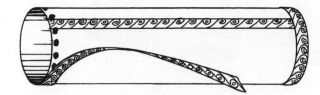

Diagram 1.
Glue braid along seam and around top

78

Window Blind *

Materials

Off-white, suit-weight fabric, 34 × 24 ins
Ring frame
Finished size: 30 × 20 ins
Appleton's Crewel Wool
2 skeins each of:
Dull Marine Blue 328
Bright China Blue 748
Cornflower 462
Sky Blue 562
1 skein of:
Cornflower 463

Instructions

Mark centre of the fabric with running
stitches, worked vertically and horizontally.
Enlarge the design and transfer to fabric.
Follow the chart overleaf and colour and
stitch keys, working the heavy buttonhole
branches with 3 strands; the stem and chain
stitch filling with 2 strands; 3 strands for
the couched leaves in colour 462, tying in
position with 1 strand; 2 strands for the
seeding and stems; and the centre of the
leaves with 3 strands. For the eyelets, work
satin stitch in a circle into the same centre
point, pulling tightly so that a hole is
formed. When complete, press on wrong side.

Making Up

Have the embroidery made up commercially
as a window blind. To make up as a
permanent flat curtain to hide an ugly view,
stitch curtain tape at the top and a dowel
rod into the bottom hem to hold the
blind flat, see diagram opposite.

Stitch Key

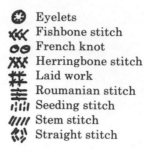

- 🞮 Buttonhole wheel
- ⬤ Chain stitch
- ⊹ Couching stitch
- ✸ Eyelets
- ⪡⪡⪡ Fishbone stitch
- ⚬⚬ French knot
- ✕✕✕ Herringbone stitch
- 🞮 Laid work
- ≣ Roumanian stitch
- ⅲⅲⅰ Seeding stitch
- ⫽⫽⫽⫽ Stem stitch
- ⫶⫶ Straight stitch

Colour Key

1–328 Marine Blue
2–748 Bright China Blue
3–462 Cornflower
4–562 Sky Blue
5–463 Cornflower

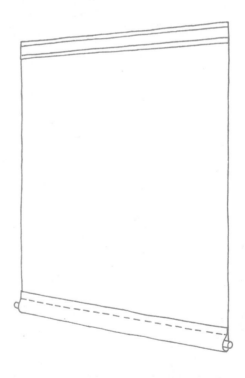

*Designed by Margaret Beautement, worked by the
Dorothy Kendall Group*

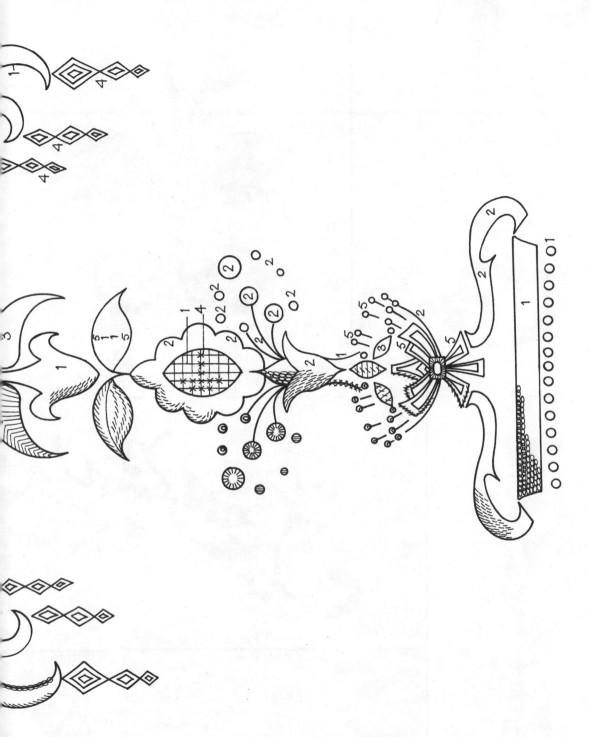

83

Motif Selection

Here we have an exciting selection of motifs for you to use singly or as a repeat pattern on any garment or material you like.

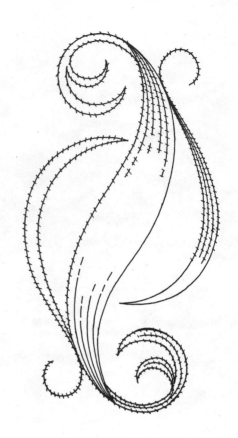

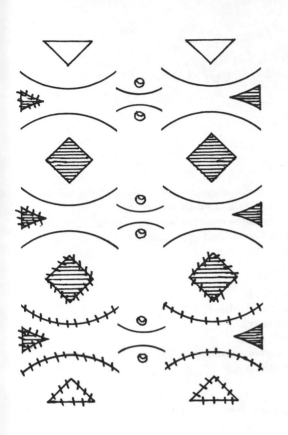

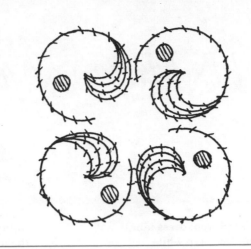

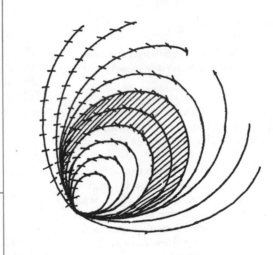

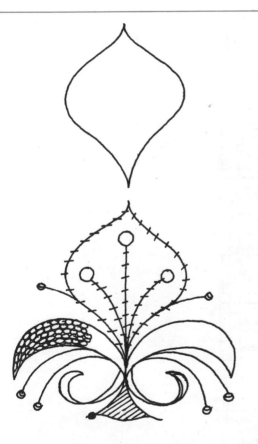

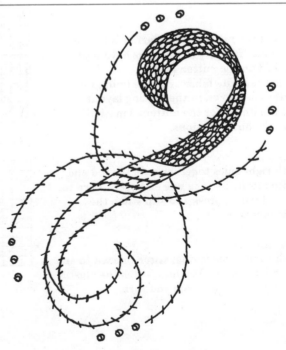

Child's Mittens and Scarf

Materials

½ yd of fine red wool dress fabric
½ yd similar fabric in white
Finished sizes: Scarf, 7 × 35 ins. Mittens, to
fit 6-year-old
Appleton's Crewel Wool
1 skein 992 off-white
A small length of contrast colour for the eye
Elastic – sufficient to fit wrists loosely

Instructions

First of all draw out paper patterns from
the graph pattern below and with tailor's
chalk mark the mitten shapes on the red
fabric.
Transfer the unicorn heads to the mittens
so that they face one another on the right
and left gloves. Cut the scarf 36 × 8 ins wide.
Transfer the unicorn to one end of the
scarf. Position it about 2 ins from one end.
Using a single strand, follow the chart
overleaf and key for stitches and colours.
Press on wrong side.

Making Up

Cut out the mittens and scarf in both red
and white fabric. ¼ in turnings have been
allowed on the mitten pattern.
From the white fabric, cut the lining for the
mittens as shown in the cutting layout.
Cut the lining for the mittens ¼ in smaller
than the outer sections.

The scarf

With right sides together, join the red and
white fabric, leaving one end open. Turn to
the right side, press and slip stitch the
ends together.

The mittens

With right sides facing, stitch one white and
one red together. Machine stitch the elastic
at the wrist. Trim seam and turn.

Stitch the linings and press. Insert the
lining, wrong sides together and slip stitch
the inner and outer sections together at
the wrist.

Stitch Key

- ▬▬ Back stitch
- ✪ Buttonhole wheel
- ⬤⬤⬤ Chain stitch
- ⬤ French knots
- ✗✗✗ Herringbone stitch
- ╫╫╫ Stem stitch

Colour Key

All embroidery – 992
Contrasting colour for eye

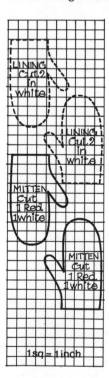

LINING
Cut 2
in
white

LINING
Cut 2
in
white

MITTEN
Cut
1 Red
1 white

MITTEN
Cut
1 Red
1 white

1 sq = 1 inch

*Designed by Margaret Beautement, worked by
Elizabeth Manley*

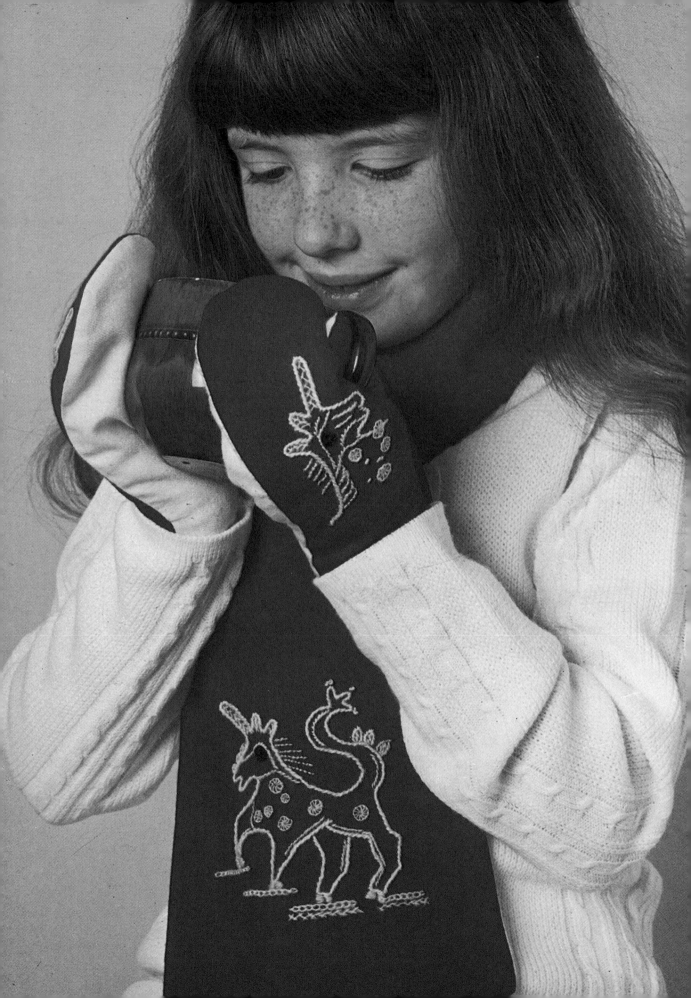

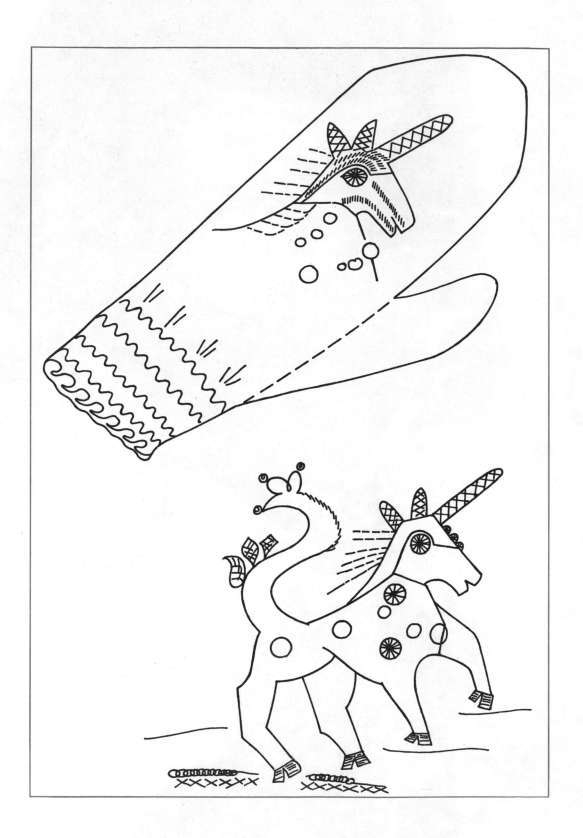

Bedspread

Materials

5½ yds by 48 ins wide of medium weight furnishing material, washable and crease resisting in cream colour
2½ yds by 48 ins wide of same material in contrasting colour (golden brown or of choice).
4 yds by 48 ins wide lining of matching main colour
8 yds by 2¾ ins wide fringing of matching main colour
Matching sewing threads
Rectangular floor frame, size 30 ins tape
Final size of single bedspread 9 × 6 ft
Appleton's Crewel Wool
6 skeins of:
Red Fawn 305
5 skeins of:
Autumn Yellow 478
4 skeins each of:
Red Fawn 304
Grey Green 352
Autumn Yellow 476
3 skeins each of:
Red Fawn 303
Drab Green 333
Grey Green 354, 355
Autumn Yellow 473, 475
Heraldic Gold 843
Putty Grounding 986
2 skeins each of:
Mid Olive Green 342, 345
Grey Green 356
Autumn Yellow 474, 479
Bright Yellow 556
Heraldic Gold 841
Putty Grounding 982
1 skein each of:
Mid Blue 154, 155
Flame Red 204, 206
Drab Green 331
Autumn Yellow 477
Peacock Blue 643, 645
Putty Grounding 981
Crewel embroidery needle, medium-size

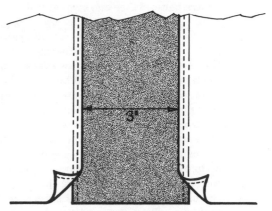

Diagram 1. Placing panels and strip to make fold

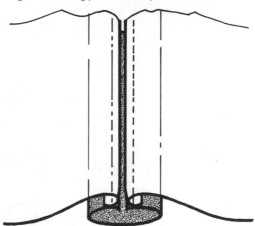

Diagram 2. Folding panels into a pleat

Instructions

Cut the 5½ yds of main material in half, giving 2 pieces of 2¾ yds each. Cut one piece to a 31 ins width panel for the centre, the other into 2 of 21½ ins width each for the side panels. Enlarge design and transfer to centre panel (31 ins). Find centre of material, place design 6½ ins away from the lower edge of the material, making sure that the centre of the design meets up with the centre of the material.
Embroider with one strand throughout. Follow chart and key for colour and

stitches. Press on wrong side.

Making Up

(All seams should be pressed after each stage.)
Cut 2 strips of the contrasting material 3 ins wide to the required length of the centre panel. Place one strip at the side edge of the panel, right sides up, tack and sew (see Diagram 1). Take one side panel (21 ins) and attach to contrasting strip in the same way. Fold the 2 raw edges of the main material under, until both panels meet, tack and stitch $\frac{3}{8}$ in away from edge into place. This forms a pleat and leaves the contrasting material just visible (see Diagram 2). Attach the other outer panel to the centre panel in the same way. Cut a strip of the main colour material of required length widthwise to fit along the top part of the bedspread, placing right sides together, and baste. Turn strip under and stitch with slip stitches into place, thus completing the head-part of the bedspread. Now complete outer edge as follows.

Cut 2 strips of contrasting material 4 ins wide to fit all round the lower edges of the bedspread. Place the 2 outer edges of the strip right sides together and sew together, turn right sides up, baste the two edges together close to the seam. This forms a double strip, the under strip being part of the finished article. Now place top strip raw edge to main edge, right sides together, baste and sew into position. Turn and fold main colour edge over the contrasting one, as shown in Diagram 2 leaving exactly 3 ins of the contrasting coloured strip free. Baste and sew into position, making sure that the under strip has been put into place and stitched together with the rest. Place fringing close to edge of fold, leaving the contrasting material just $\frac{1}{4}$ in visible (see Diagram 3).
Cut the lining in half widthwise, sew selvedges together, thus putting the seam horizontal when fitting the lining into position. Bring edges of lining to within the edge of the contrasting material, turn raw edges and slip stitch into position.

92

Stitch Key

ℴℴ	Single open buttonhole stitch
ℴℴℴ	Double open buttonhole stitch
✕✕	Cross stitch
ℴℴ	Detached chain stitch
ℽℽ	Twisted chain stitch
∞∞	Whipped chain stitch
ℇℇ	Single feather stitch
⋘	Fishbone stitch
✕✕	Open fishbone stitch
≫	Fly stitch
⋎⋎	Detached fly stitch
ℴℴ	French knots
⫽⫽⫽⫽	Satin stitch
⫶⫶⫶	Seeding
⊹⊹⊹	Stem stitch
=⫽	Straight stitch
⍺	Wheatear stitch

Colour Key

(Check colour numbers by referring to materials, page 91.)

1–303	9–478	17–342	25–154
2–304	10–479	18–345	26–155
3–305	11–352	19–841	27–204
4–473	12–354	20–843	28–206
5–474	13–355	21–981	29–643
6–475	14–356	22–982	30–645
7–476	15–331	23–986	
8–477	16–333	24–556	

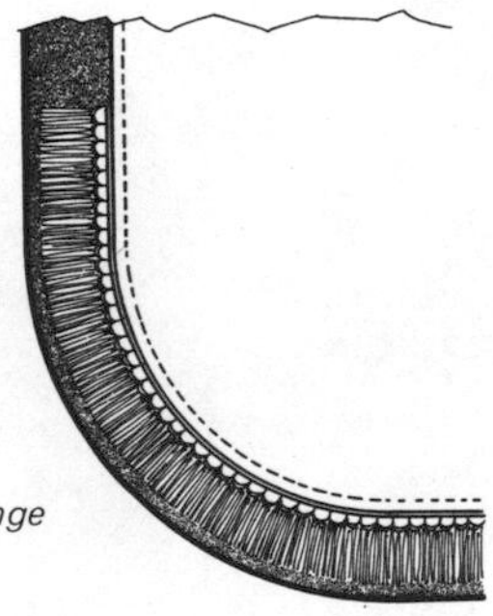

Diagram 3. Bedspread showing fringe over contrast edging ▶

93